T0368221

PRESENT MOMENT,
PERFECT MOMENT

KATHLEEN KEENA, LPC, LADC

PRESENT MOMENT, PERFECT MOMENT

Copyright © 2020 KATHLEEN KEENA, LPC, LADC.

All rights reserved. No part of this book may be used or reproduced by any means, graphic, electronic, or mechanical, including photocopying, recording, taping or by any information storage retrieval system without the written permission of the author except in the case of brief quotations embodied in critical articles and reviews.

All illustrations are created by **Kathleen Keena, LPC, LADC**

iUniverse books may be ordered through booksellers or by contacting:

iUniverse
1663 Liberty Drive
Bloomington, IN 47403
www.iuniverse.com
1-800-Authors (1-800-288-4677)

Because of the dynamic nature of the Internet, any web addresses or links contained in this book may have changed since publication and may no longer be valid. The views expressed in this work are solely those of the author and do not necessarily reflect the views of the publisher, and the publisher hereby disclaims any responsibility for them.

ISBN: 978-1-6632-0460-8 (sc)
978-1-6632-0461-5 (e)

Library of Congress Control Number: 2020912154

Print information available on the last page.

iUniverse rev. date: 07/13/2020

PRESENT MOMENT,
PERFECT MOMENT

KATHLEEN KEENA, LPC, LADC

241 South Water Street, Unit 3
East Windsor, Ct. 06088

860-623-6587

Kathykeena54@gmail.com

CHAPTER ONE:
TIME

CHAPTER ONE:
TIME

TIME

I am the trajectory, time
propelling change.

The shape shifting energy
that must, that will.

I combust,
I grow and decay;
the wave you ride,
the freezeless frame.

I am collusion,
the random unseen,
the anonymous, possible,
refracted beam.

* * * * *

MEMORIALS

Memorials are flares
we shoot into the dark.
lit up momentarily,
then lost.

Memorials never measure
how much grief
subtracts from us.

Like walking
on a beach
of finely ground sand,
shifting, changing,
sifting through hands.

❊   ❊   ❊   ❊   ❊

IT IS TIME THAT TAKES AWAY

All of the roads,
the factories,
created by blood
of our common ancestry.

The desire to own the Connecticut
stole the river away
from Poquonock tribes
honoring
the sacred river.

Past century streets,
settler buildings
stand vacantly.
No horse drawn carriages,
or mud slick paths
now paved streets
eroding fast.
The water reclaims
the past.

An angry fort
on coastline beach
stands courageously.
Inside stone walls
a grass bed
reclaims ownership.

No one takes a life away,
it is time that steals us
from today.

Through stretching
uncertainty
Native Americans
fished and trapped.
Puritans put
a halt to that.

Connecticut carpet lords
exchanged profit
for toxic death,
a rich yield.

Mothers cried
when harsh winters stole
their babies' lives.

And what we wish for,
why we cry,
is gone before
our dwellings die.

Why we are angry,
why alone,
no one will know
or care to know.

* * * * *

TOPPS, 1965

Saturdays, circa 1965,
Dad would jump
into the driver's seat
of the Ford Flacon.
Johnny and I
sat in back,
driving to Topps.

Topps smelled of bubbling grease
with deep fried dough.
floating O's.
We smelled the congealing
sugar sauce
coating the donuts
we'd never eat.

* * * * *

Dad and John
rushing to auto care,
buying oil, filters,
motorcycle repair,
while I,
clutching babysitting money
rushed to outfit
eleven and a half inch alters.

Dolls who never knew
chafing hose,
ill-fitting clothes,
arms bleeding in the cold,
frizzy unkept hair.

Dolls who would get an A
in English, later an A
on the parallel bars.

Dolls whose painted smiles,
elongated bodies
stretching disproportionately
into the sky,
dolls who always won,
who never cried.

✳   ✳   ✳   ✳   ✳

BIG KIDS

Racing bikes down
Windsor Avenue,
I, behind you,
speeding toward
Windsor Center.

We, the big kids
of the family,
stayed up late,
and, in 1964,
saw The Beatles
at the Plaza in
Hard Day's Night.

Tiptoeing through
Wilson library,
tutoring you
in academic reverence.

We loved to share
funny stuff.
We both thought
we'd share funny, forever.

Instead, my brother,
you flew into the blue
while I so sharply missing you.

*   *   *   *   *

THE CULTURE OF THE BONNET DRYER

Growing cowlicks
where they never
ought to have grown,

Shirley Temple
was never my mother,
I had to face this alone.

My mother brought me
to Alice's shop,
who praised my curls.
Looking down the aisle
I saw, single file,
hair dryer bonnets;
martian moons.

Jane's head
hidden under
a massive insect hive.
Her glasses off,
I gasped, I coughed;
what cruel crime
Was she enduring?

I was led to a chair,
cranked high
and locked.
So, how did I want
my bangs?
We need to lose the length;
an unbecoming mess,
crabgrass, in fact.

Yes. Okay.
Okay, yes.

At least I was not shoved
under the shame
of the bonnet dryer.

I had wanted to look
like Judy Garland
in Wizard of Oz,
instead, my head
became Lady Birds'.

Oh boy, I thought.
I will never
beautify America.

❊   ❊   ❊   ❊   ❊

DECKER BROOK

We'd meet at the corner of Legion
and Decker Brook,
where stout rats scrambled so fast
only their long tails
switched under the bridge.

This was before the town
lay concrete down,
installing the new
Attractive Bridge,
Without missing planks
or trash lined banks.
This was well before that.

My day would depend
on the level of pain
the torture curlers
created that night.

※　※　※　※　※

You, with your swan's neck
and tall grace,
me, chubby, short,
in braces and ill-fitting clothes,
rumpled dress
and bouncing curls
refusing to be combed.

We used to wear hose
that left our thighs so
frozen cold that
steely junior high doors
opened to fresh warmth.

* * * * *

END OF CHILDHOOD

Captain Action
transcended space and time;
fought in the Peloponnesian Wars
with distinction.

World War Two,
on a submarine,
he carried his comrades
to safety
from blazing ships.

In the jungles of Vietnam
it was rumored Vietcong
sought to challenge him
as a worthy foe.

Captain Action
was more than a toy
to the boy who shadowed him
through unimaginable danger,
and survived.

* * * * *

Captain Action,
in the cellar at night, sleeping,
would remain incognito
until needed.

He might be found
guarding a window or door
from harsher elements,
holding back storms
with his mighty arms.

Not only did he captain his actions,
he was a model of humanity.
He could see pain
in the face of an enemy
and feel compassion.

The one who stayed with
a dying man, holding his hand
until final breath.

Then, without warning,
Captain Action disappeared.
a classified mission
was presumed.

Searching the house by day,
wandering alone,
the boy asked everyone
if they had seen his Captain.

Then, his brother
beckoned him
into their room.
Do you want to know
where your little dollie went?

He showed a video
of two road racers,
one perishing in a fire.

Close up on tod Captain Action
unconscious and burning
in the fiery crash,
his plastic flesh melting,
his uniform burned
from his body,
dying alone.

His brother laughed.
Horror hit.
The boy ran into the backyard,
blaming himself,
heartbroken,
helpless to save
his cherished friend.

This was the end
of everything.

* * * * *

GHOSTS

Before Arlo had a head of silver,
forty kids and grandkids,
Windsor High hippies
spent Saturday nights
listening to him announce
the New York Freeway is closed, man!
Our mantra.

My boyfriend and I,
both with dark,
shoulder length hair,
surreptitiously discovering
FM radio
at his kitchen table,
The Woodstock album
burned into our memory.

Forty years later,
driving through
The New York Freeway.
the flooded plain,
the pounding rain, the mud,
reminding me.

Because, today,
The New York Freeway
is without shoulders,
emergency stopping only.
fifteen hundred feet.

Driving the old imperfect road,
we see a concrete one,
freshly poured,
parallel to us.
Disarming.
but,
between the two roads,
a mud drenched range,
and shadows of ghosts
dance to reclaim
Woodstock.

* * * * *

HEY, ROD STEWART

I was there as you pranced across
the New Haven Colosseum stage, 1973.
an ambitious peacock
of ambiguous sexuality.

I wrapped my life
around reason to believe,
at seventeen
becoming Maggie May
I flew on a
transcontinental plane
to London.

The feather boa
that fluttered
when you moved,
the spiky haircut,
the purple shoes,
and that voice of yours,
expressing all the longing
in the universe.

Hey Rod Stewart
I followed you
on Mandolin winds,
your edgy voice slicing
under my skin,
singing all I knew,
if I listened long enough to you.

* * * * *

MAUSOLEUM

A mausoleum shrouds
the relics of my past.

The girl in that photo;
eyes bright with curiosity,
shaking off all that is not
liberty.

Licenses,
handsomely framed,
require more training
to sustain.
Although no longer practicing
professionally,
I want my name in a frame.

Traveler, writer,
theater artist.
The mausoleum
of my past.
Entombed in memory.

*   *   *   *   *

WHAT WAS SAID

Love is a terrible thing,
he said,
sitting at the head
of the table.

Never get old, Kath,
he advised,
smoking the perpetual cigarette
with the black plastic tip,
thought to catch the worst
of the tar.

People don't like old people,
he told me,
while I nodded passively.

Was this code
to surrender?

❅   ❅   ❅   ❅   ❅

BEHIND CERTAIN DOORS

Behind certain doors,
permanently latched,
I see slivers of light
shifting past.

And on such nights,
and through such cracks,
I take a breath
and make my way.

There to find
a rack of clothes,
an attic stashed
with crates of toys,
perhaps a lost doll.

Or, people rushing to lecture,
having recently,
urgently, published.

Sometimes corridors, stairwells
Or bombed out streets,
echoes of small,
desperate feet.

The long yawn
of before
meets the present tense
Of my breath.

* * * * *

AND SO THE BLUE

Then, a suburban girl,
front counter clerk,
you were older, bolder.

You told me
when your father hit you,
you'd smile
and lift your chin
a little higher.

I loved your defiance.

The Connecticut river,
whose silent banks,
water roads,
bathed our feet
in cool, forgiving flow.

And so the blue.
And so the green.
And so the crickets.
And so the dream.

❋   ❋   ❋   ❋   ❋

BAD ATTITUDE

When our kayak
was stolen,
the summer sun,
previously benevolent,
became an irritant.

Simultaneously,
we lost power. Stranded.
Unable to cook,
shower, or wash clothes.

And we both felt...
undermined.
Despite knowing
this can and does
happen to so many,
involuntarily.

And we had
the opportunity
to appreciate our blessings.

But no.
Neither of us took it
patiently.
We knocked around
in the dark.
We grumbled,
uncharitably.

✳   ✳   ✳   ✳   ✳

WORDS

I was living on a strip of rock,
curling around a jagged shore.
Words hurled over me,
sea waves.

Stop the words!
Stop the words!
You can't stop us! they cried.

They leapt over everything,
like seafoam they rushed
to inhabit my life.

The house was waterlogged
in metaphors
and still those damn words
kept crashing.
Sea spray broke over
word soaked windows.

WOULD YOU MIND!
I screamed.
Wetly, I watch them
wash out to sea.
That soggy shack
of overworked words
and me.

❋ ❋ ❋ ❋ ❋

CHAPTER TWO:
NATURAL WORLD

CHAPTER TWO:
NATURAL WORLD

WAVES

Tall, straight grass
parting like the strands
of a women's locks,
collapsing back in waves,
ample, lush,
flowing down the shoulders
of the forest.

* * * * *

DEBUTANTES

They come out shyly,
debutantes,
in palest shades of pink.

Citrus green
fledgling buds
poking out
against a blue,
cloudless sky.

Dandelion roots
plunge like pipelines
to middle earth.

Willows, lime
begin to droop,
delicate leaves,
butterflies.

Hearty stalks,
rhododendron bushes
flash yellow alarms
along the highway
where we walk.

✳   ✳   ✳   ✳   ✳

MIRROR IN WATER

Mirrored canal,
mid-September,
early morning
forest breathing.

Inhale, exhale
water leaves wave
upside down.

In such a sacred place
of rest,
Narcissus fell,
lovestruck,
on the framing riverbank
the fluid world below.

Branches
under glass.
He gazes down
into an endlessly
deep world
of inverse light.

He cannot
look away.

❋   ❋   ❋   ❋

LEAVES IN AUGUST

Late August,
deep green turning trees
wave arms
to darker skies.

Waving goodbye,
they remain
rustling, throwing
wide spreading shade
across parched lawns
absent rain.

Such trees,
survivors of harsher days;
the ice, snow,
frozen limbs,
winter's persistent ground
pushing down.

In August,
trees, fully dressed,
gracefully
wave into fall.

❊ ❊ ❊ ❊ ❊

Suddenly, the Frost

It used to arrive
early October,
scraping my windshield,
collecting confetti
colored leaves.

On Halloween,
marigolds,
and those perky red stalks;
who could suppose
they would remain,
sixty, seventy degrees.

Unfettered gardens
blooming,
ignoring the season
long overdue,
grass still green.

Short sleeves,
an alien fall
for Connecticut.
Trees arrested
in August green;
only rain loosens leaves.

They say no more snow
for us, while Southern California.
forests blaze.

They say it was the work
of an eleven-year old.
I say we had
something to do with it.

Suddenly, in November
like an afterthought,
the frost.
Too late for migrant birds
to fly.

Retail stores
paint snow
on windows,
Christmas music
piping low.

* * * * *

As the Wind

As the wind
tears leaves
from tree limbs,
standing thin like
the arms of the oldest
In a nursing home.

As the wind
reaches in
to take hold,
enfolding breath,
hanging in clouds
before us,
stealing summer
like a crumbling home.

❋　❋　❋　❋　❋

WINDOW

A rare precious bird
flew through
my window one night,
his feathers sleek and smooth.

On his breast,
purple scars
weaved trails
from earlier wounds.

Strange princely bird,
rest from flight.

Fly through
the open window
of my life.

✳   ✳   ✳   ✳   ✳

WILD LOVE

Dreaming of safety and wildness
the water tosses your hair
into curls.

Rustling leaves
lean into you
and I dream
of endlessly falling
into layers of
fantastic netting,
spinning, glistening
golden threads.

I sleep
in your arms.
Darkness washes us,
all is fluid.
Your breath, the air.

❋   ❋   ❋   ❋   ❋

MORNING SWIM

Night sky
through glass,
clear water below.
Gentle splash.
Weightless dive.

Next,
the sliding,
rhythmic glide.

Swimming, I am
a beam of light
moving through
night's shadows.

✳   ✳   ✳   ✳   ✳

WALK WITH ME

Walk with me,
the forest damp, or dry.
The wind urgent,
or clearing sky.

Carpets of moss,
obstinately green,
water flowing
stormy streams.

Spirit shadows
in the leaves,
their song calls
to echo in me.

❊   ❊   ❊   ❊   ❊

SLICE OF ORANGE

The moon,
a slice of orange,
floats in a sea
of black.

Dark December
twilight,
as black as ink,
as cold as black.

I drive
through the night,
ice falling
through hidden cracks.

The slice of orange,
the only light
penetrates
solid night.

✻　✻　✻　✻　✻

PRECISE COAT

Winter round low sunset
balances above
the river.

Trees, luminous light
painting smooth,
gold strands
streaming through
sleeping branches.

Frozen in snow,
whiter in sunlight.

White meadows glow,
embracing homes,
climbing abandoned
backyard ladders,
unvarnished planks
of summer decks.

Resting on steps or
across clothing
left too long on the line,
draping the groundling scrubs.

This precise coat
paints all things fresh,
foreign, mysterious.

❋   ❋   ❋   ❋   ❋

TO SWIM

When the river begins
and ocean ends
when moon hangs low
as dead leaves spin,
and rocks stand straight
against the wind,
the night we met,
summer's end.

When autumn shades
each empty face,
sunlight falls early
into space,
when dead husks roll
On sandy land,
You gave your love to me.

You of the shadow world
where phantoms ride
on strong, full wind
come gallop with
as sirens sing.

I will steer you away,
I will teach you to swim.

❋ ❋ ❋ ❋ ❋

WATERLINE

I dreamed last night
the sea crept
to our basement door,
the waterline
frighteningly high.

While other swam
or boated,
we stayed in.

Close the curtains!
I said.
And the wind,
perpetual wind.

Our theater, dark,
on the opposite side.
Relentless wind,
pushing the door in,
the water invading
our home, our skin.

* * * * *

MOONBEAM

Blanketed in darkness
as others sleep,
you steal, moonbeam,
to me.

Slipping off your shoes,
in the half light,
you arrive.

I know you.
Perfectly wrong.
Gracefully awkward.
Foolishly strong.

And yet,
your silhouette
remains.

❋   ❋   ❋   ❋   ❋

CANAL PATH

Great whitecapped
mushrooms
line the bank
of the Locks.

They took the trees away
that did not survive
the heaviest snow.
No one heard
Their great spirits go.

In April we found ourselves
walking the Locks, again.
A panoramic,
unobstructed view
of the canal
straight through
the farther shore.

In our yard,
A dog sized beaver
clutches a stick.
The beaver will not
loosen its' grip.

He stands, frozen,
on hind legs
waiting for the
invisible escape path.

✳   ✳   ✳   ✳   ✳

STRANGE SUMMER

The rain ran
the river high.
Draining grass.
now dust dry.

No one could believe
it was July,
the air so cold
we wore
our winter coats.

No halter tops,
no bare-chested men
chewing gum,
leaning on cars.

None.
Strange Summer.

* * * * *

NO SNOW FALLS

No snow falls
on the western plain.
desert sun rises early,
stays late.

The gardens grow
in heat and sand.

Deprived lives
do not cry.

Only the sun,
the ruler sun,
swallows the dust
relentlessly.

The empty air
escapes
through my hands.

❋   ❋   ❋   ❋   ❋

CHAPTER THREE:
LOSS

CHAPTER THREE:

LOSS

You Know Who I Am

I am the master of escape
I drive without lights
in the blackout lane.
I am vapor dissolving
at dawn.
I am the absence
you may count on.

I am the shadow
on your fire escape,
I am the path you will take.
I am the tears
you will weep
I am the dream
you may not keep.

I am the last illusion
you will hold.

You Know Who I Am.

* * * * *

LOSS IS A GARMENT

Loss is a garment
worn under the skin.
Seeping inside,
dissolving through
flesh, organs, bones.

Loss is a garment
worn as a scar,
unseen,
in charge,
unkempt.

* * * * *

GAZING BOWL

Flight.
Then, blinding hurt,
unexpected loss.

Two hummingbirds transfixed
in a gazing bowl
of their own bath
now smash
through the sheer glass
of death.

Mistaken for air,
unaware
the lacquered glass
conceals edges
to tear wings.
To rip bones.
Eager to swallow
life whole.

* * * * *

I GRIEVE

He told me I had
a difficult time
letting things go.
It is true,
but is it wrong?

And your brothers
are just like you.
and your father,
he was like that, too.

I was quiet.
I did not disagree.

Why do you hang on
like that, he asked.

I grieve my dead friends,
dead family,
lost employment,
identity.

I grieve the loss
of health.
A speedy mind.
The belief in some
grand design.

I grieve for loss
Of stamina,
I grieve for us
killing the planet.

I grieve for the soldiers
who won't return,
I grieve for their families
opening doors
into emptiness.

Yes.
I guess
I have trouble with that.

* * * * *

UNTREATED

We carry the untreated wounds
of our parents
on our backs,
in our blood.

They transfer to us
through lifetimes
of thoughtlessness.

Sometimes,
we become the wounds.
The wounds that hide.

They tell our parents
To say
its okay, when it's not.
They tell us to hide
what most intimately
expresses our humanity.

The disappointments,
regrets, inside.
And we never know
if it is us or them
we carry.

The spine may collapse,
supporting the weight
of such heavy packs.

*   *   *   *   *

HEAR YOUR ABSENCE

I can still hear
the creaking door,
your soft step
climbing the stair,
the touch of your hands
on my hips,
your gentle kiss
waking me.

In dark, subterranean
consciousness,
your hand pressed on
the small of my back,
my fingers twine
through your silky hair,
eternally safe.

Abruptly,
your final breath.
The ashes of your remains
sift through
my empty heart.

Still,
I hear you.

❋ ❋ ❋ ❋ ❋

WATER, SAND, FRAGILITY

As water seeks the sea,
as violence seeks
complacency,
we walk through shadows
of uncertainty.

The thin thread
that weaves our lives,
a spiderweb
of fragile strands;
a bloodstained hand
still feels
the salt, the sand.

Wounds attach
to us
like barnacles,
they cover us,
they hold us back,
Seeking comfort.

*   *   *   *   *

THE EDGES OF GOODBYE

A memorial kiss
the precarious place
of cavernous alone,
rushes in to freeze
any heart naïve
to believe
love remains.

A wave of emptiness,
vast as ocean,
replaces
the certain permanent.

✳   ✳   ✳   ✳   ✳

Molecules in space,
moving, directionless,
yet forward,
shed superfluous.

Here's how love
changes us.
It burns away
all we are not,
it seeks and finds
truth.

It is what we feel,
think and resist.
It burns and scars.
It is why we exist.

✳   ✳   ✳   ✳   ✳

THE BUSINESS OF DEATH

Mother Courage was right.
there is profit in death.

The oxygen tanks,
tall as sentries
guard the hospital bed
beside a nightstand of
CPAP, hygienic gloves, wipes,
breathing mask.

The living room
transforms
to room of death.

Commodities
of death
occupy the space.

Wheelchair, walker,
hover lift,
automatic chairs
control our schedules,
arrange our days.

The man in the bed
is small.
He has his part to play.

The machines surrounding him
command center stage.

❋   ❋   ❋   ❋   ❋

I Did Not Bear It Bravely

I did not bear it bravely
when you left the room.
Lost petals of flowers,
left on the ground.

Thanksgiving from
another room.

Children calling,
who still need you.

Don't say I am brave.

If your loved one
was leaving you,
you would also howl
In hopelessness,
as all living creatures do.

In agony.
Silently tremendous.

❋   ❋   ❋   ❋   ❋

LUCID DREAMING

And I am so positive
I am in my childhood bed,
my father's motorcycle
roaring closer,
the thud, thud, thud
of the motor winding down.

The garage door opens.
He walks his warhorse
to its'stall.
Before he closes
the garage door,
I fall asleep again.

Or my brother and I
in our new house,
and we're the big kids.
We're tuned into a frequency
only we can hear,
always on the edge of laughter.

Spring whispering through
dining room windows
mingle with far off voices.
One deeper,
the other faster,
clipping along.
A radio almost off,
always on.

* * * * *

THIRTY-FIVE

He will always be thirty-five,
slightly balding,
not yet gray.

He will always have
the angular jaw,
bursting like sunlight
into a smile,
delighted to amuse.

A definite preference
for the ridiculous;
a Special Forces
wild card.

He had to be crazy
to fly those certain
suicide missions,
who else would rescue
wounded
in enemy camps
as if riding a ferris wheel?

Overprotecting us,
I never knew how dangerous
it was to be selfless,
thirty-five,
and smiling.

* * * * *

STRUGGLE TO BE STILL

My father's dilapidated frame,
having lately succumbed to death,
wore no lingering regret
or held on a moment beyond
death's call.

He exited that day
a willing participant
departing pain.
Death relieved him
the difficulty of breath,
leaving us
an aged, broken frame
once containing
A giant.

Only one so
perilously present
could be so absolutely
absent.

For him and for all
of us
who live too close
to the bone,
although releasing
to nature's will,
it is a mighty struggle
to be still.

❊   ❊   ❊   ❊   ❊

YOU NEVER CAME BACK

The unwashed dishes
in your sink,
caked with tomato sauce.

Your unmade bed,
pillows untossed,
your dusty floors,
open doors,
cupboards stocked;
oatmeal, peanut butter, tuna.

Your half-written journals,
your open books,
the black lacquered table
with white garden chairs,
where we shared
so many meals.

Surely, surely
you'd be back,
to finish that laundry,
to get your mail,
to buy tofetti,
to hear the train roar
past open windows.
The soundtrack

of your life.
We would float to sleep
as it clanked by.

You'd be back,
so we could laugh,
burning candles into
the night,
whispering through
some play we'd seen,
or like to produce;
how we would plan
costume, stage
and light.

In the morning you'd whisper
are you awake?
Peering from under
your sheets.

And I,
in the single bed
across from you
opened my eyes
to see your smile.

You'd be back,
I knew.

* * * * *

HOLLYWOOD TO PASADENA

Thirty-two years
is too brief, dear friend,
to steal us
from each other.

From the boulevard
of Hollywood
to Pasanda storefront
we were reason
enough to survive.

Now death.

Pacific waves
call you back,
so soft, so clean,
so unattached.
Like those waves,
we never
owned each other.

Yet like tangled seaweed,
our lives blended
together,
one shimmering necklace
of life.

And your bravery.
Who else would say no
to psych meds,
identify healthcare
inequities,
advocate
patient autonomy
decades before
equal access.

Who else could play
Mother Courage,
hauling her wagon
through fields of graves.

From belly laughs
celebrating absurdity,
walking down
Hollywood Boulevard.
Who else but you,
dear friend
would find
such an expedient end?

❋   ❋   ❋   ❋   ❋

GRIEF IS NOW MY SISTER

Walking arm in arm
through Cambridge,
thrift shopping or
stopping for
frozen yogurt,
grief is now my sister.

She's a lot like you.
Warmer, wiser than me.
My sister self
walks ahead,
urging me
to the next block,
where we'll rest.

Teaching me to step
when I'm stopped,
to understand why
I hide;
how briefly we live,
how soon we die.

Grief is now my sister,
my new best friend,
sometimes dropping down
to quicksand, or
in hypnotic dream,
we fly
into infinity.
My new sister and I
walk arm in arm,
carrying our love for you
like beats in a measure,
drops of rain
falling to earth
to be soaked up again.

❊　❊　❊　❊　❊

TO CRY

To cry is to undress emotionally.
The rape of rationality,
between the lines
A and B.

I was a wounded animal
the day you died,
stifling my
hound dog wail.

Why do we cry?
It seizes
the mask of everyone.
Steals the most guarded
roles we play.

The day of your funeral,
the tears, the sweat,
I was wet,
I was left,
a soggy sheet
of tissue mashed
and crumbling.

✳ ✳ ✳ ✳ ✳

HOLOGRAPH

I go into drugstore now
looking for you.
One night I dreamt you
lived in a round store,
curving, curving.
Between aisles of seasonal
and the loading dock,
I found you.

Whatever you're doing,
I wonder how
you're doing it
and from now until Christmas
you'll have no time
for anything
except the store.
The back door.
I am looking for you.

I find myself peering
around the next endcap,
listening for you.
A holographic image,
you will always be
in these aisles,
the small appliances,
the health and beauty aids.
Dangling the keys
to everything.

You taught me to drape
garland around artificial trees.
You, in hushpuppies,
soundless.
The basement stairs
diving down
into endless overstock.

The many hours,
Waiting, waiting,
wanting so much to learn
whatever it was
I was apprenticing for.

*   *   *   *   *

CHAPTER FOUR:
SOCIAL ISSUES

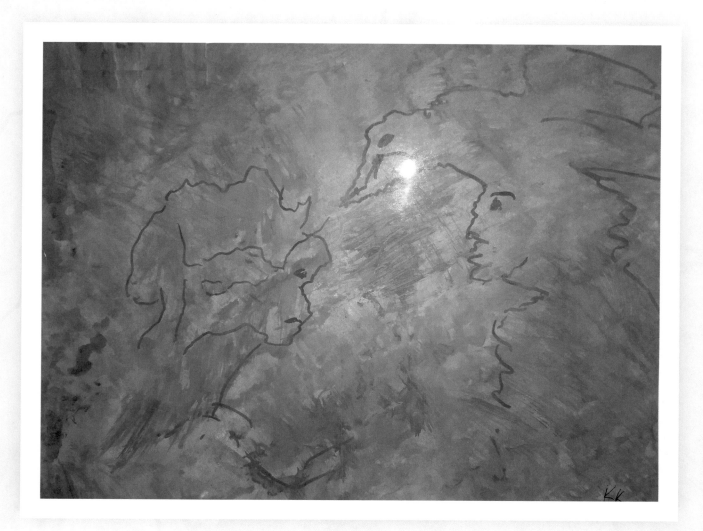

85

SOCIAL ISSUES

ANTHONY SURRENDERS

Anthony surrenders to Cleopatra
even after she twice deserts him.
Looking into her face,
he knows
wherever she goes,
he follows.

Anthony surrenders to
the consuming need
of Cleopatras'
to be needed.

The Cleopatra
Anthony knows
betrayed him twice
In battle.

Then, feigning death,
sends word to Anthony,
who wounds himself,
mortally.

❋   ❋   ❋   ❋   ❋

RICHARD THE THIRD

Shakespeare's Richard the Third,
fated at birth,
the worse tyrant in William's sphere,
no redeeming qualities
in his gene pool.
Contriving to steal
men's souls.

Yet all too well
do we know
the Richard the Third
within our souls:
the envious goals we compose
to thwart those
who have
what we covet.

The sad, loveless quest
that splits open the chest.
the darkest secrets we hide;
the absence of conflict
for wounds we inflict.

❄ ❄ ❄ ❄ ❄

CHARLES BUKOWSKI

An actor I was married to
used to see Charles Bukowski
early seventies,
stumbling through
downtown streets of L.A.
muttering to himself.
I don't remember if he had a bag,
but let's give him the bag.

So there he is,
blinding L.A. midday sun
over uneven sidewalks,
as another artist, the actor,
watches unseen from a window.

Bukowski's speech
staccatoed
with drunken emphasis,
rambling.

He assaults the language,
a verbal disgrace.
His rant continues.

The actor, who is drawn to
Bukowski's incoherent
self-destruction,
joins to inhabit his darkness.

✳   ✳   ✳   ✳   ✳

NEW ORLEANS FLOODS

Despite the bodies floating
face down in front yards,
despite the sloshing raw sewage,
despite the lack of drinking water,
some stayed.

They peer out the windows
of ravaged homes,
down rivers, once roads,
believing their homes
would keep them safe.

But it is not safe.
The sofa and chairs
in living rooms
are racid,
the t.v. drowned.

They remain on second floors,
roofs buckled
under water weight
or destroyed by hatchet break,
they wave for help,
abandoned.

Animals lie dead, too.
their carcasses
bloated in stench,
ninety-degree heat,
with oceans of fire
from gas leaks.

No one alive
in New Orleans
will forget the smell.

Soon, rats will come,
to own the living rooms.
Huge river rats
who know how to adapt
And thrive beside death.
They are the new owners
of the waterlogged homes.

A city of naked rat brothers
runs the
Mardigras.
Rats play Dixieland,
Mik Jagger swaggers through
Stella and Stanley's
former back porch.

What is fresh rots.
What is green, dead.
Only the unthinkable
alive.

❋   ❋   ❋   ❋   ❋

SEPTEMBER FRIDAY

We were the combustibles
of the World Trade Center.
The alibis of death,
the first to die.

There was no time to decide
why planes flying in the sky
became our
atmospheric graves.

We were the ammunition
for the annihilation that followed:
the plane nose crashing,
our bodies igniting,
a giant gray cloud
of human rain.

Not consulted,
Merely in the way.
Like talcum power,
blown
on an autumn day.

Our ashes lingered
on the skin
of witnesses.
For reporters,
our gray powder
carved out their
terrified eyes.

They wore our deaths
on their lips, tongues,
under fingernails.

The narrow stairwell
tricked firemen climbing
to become dust.

We were the campfire
that bright, clear day,
the sky, an inviting hue
while floors of offices
turned to kindling.

That was us
you were breathing
and swallowing.

Some of us jumped
to welcome death
ground zero.

✳   ✳   ✳   ✳   ✳

Each September

The air burns.

The blasting violence
of commercial planes
bursts again into flames
of the Twin Towers.

Never meant to be flown through,
a season of violence
explodes annually.

The passengers, tourists,
office workers,
those who plunged
from the highest floors,
hitting the pavement with a dull thud,
bleed through the air
of the massive crash,
New York city
a gelatin of shock.

✳   ✳   ✳   ✳   ✳

NINE ELEVEN

The moon, full.
tugging at us,
a giant hand
clutching collective sorrow.

The violence, the violation,
the victims
bound in death.

Dust of the dead
worn on skin of survivors.
Ghostly power,
startled eyes, still awake.

Hunting with dogs
for shards
of humanity.

✳   ✳   ✳   ✳   ✳

VENICE IN JUNE (APOLOGIES TO GINSBERG)

I saw the best minds of my generation
selling bongs along Venice Beach, 2006.

Street venders
bartered indigenously festive weaves,
Mexican food
served on surfboards.

I heard the best voice of my generation
shirtless on a side street,
painted in concrete.
The risen Morrison,
microphone, a sepulcher
clenched in his right hand.
He was walking
into the sun.

The man turned to myth,
high priest
of the anarchy.

You were out there looking,
just like me.
I don't feel well.
Don't bother me.

* * * * *

I am Persephone

When October sun
coaxes long shadows
across our paths,
when the trees,
hanging on to green
form an archway of arms
above the dirt road,

When what has grown
now retreats
under silent soil,
or dies,
will I be as able
to surrender?

For me, a journey through
the underworld
and I, Persephone,
full of pomegranate seed.

I step into
my bark canoe
down dark waters.
An arrangement made,
half in brilliance,
Half in shade.

In autumn we are all afraid.

❋   ❋   ❋   ❋   ❋

TSUNAMI, DAY FOUR, 140,000 DEAD

Like a fist
this mammoth water giant
punched its way to land.

Not everyone could run
to the mountains.
Some gave their lives
for footage.
Bodies underwater
by the beach resort
bright paper umbrellas
float with corpses.

Absurd things survived;
one lone dwelling stood
as the dead floated by
with drowned dogs
and wood.

The air was foul,
the bodies stank,
no one dare enter
the water of the dead
without masks.

People searched to find
what most dread,
the bodies of people
whose lives had defined their own.

* * * * *

Train Wreak
Transforms to Cash

His skill as a money machine,
mythical.
He rode the sea of bargains
like a colossus,
pulling consumers into his orbit,
a mighty magnet.

Just a splash of motor oil
and a tarnished child's toy
transformed to joy
in the nursery.

A vessel lost at sea
resurfaced treasures
in his inventory.

Crystal goblets,
dinner platters,
napkins, bowls and serving handles.

The guy had insight
into every fatality.
For every dark disaster,
he rode the train
of useful after.

✳ ✳ ✳ ✳ ✳

NEGATIVE OOOMMMM

Midnight Sun.
All he wanted was to love
and be loved.
But when the sun rose,
that palatial no man's land
sprang from the earth
into the clouds
and he dove
to the crater
of the midnight sun.

The universal life force,
the ooommm of inner peace,
drowned now by the coins
Pouring out
of slot machines.

Some may claim those
imitation streets
with phony storefronts
invited any player
justify a bet. And yet
as the alcohol poured
each thousand dollars
disappeared more easily.

The second sun
of artificial light
shone for him,
too high a price.
lost in the blindness
of the midnight sun.

❋   ❋   ❋   ❋   ❋

CORONAVIRUS

Yoga mats rolled,
gym bags of unused clothes
movie houses,
restaurants closed.

Leaving the house alone
to grocery shop
I stare at the empty
shelves of disinfectants,
toilet paper, bleach.

Fortunate artists react
with clarity articulate the grief
of loss of community.

On T.V.,
college students, invincibly
swarm beaches
in swim trunks and bikinis,
gulls screeching
like angry children
missing parents.

The bluest gray
Of the water
Breathing, heaving,
A giant lung.

Brown bodies glistening.
Contagion, unheeded.
they fly too close
to the sun.

*　*　*　*　*

VICIOUS TEETH

Late spring,
snow lingers on fallen leaves,
air saturated with killer virus,
hail falling on full blooming
Flower beds.

Masked neighbors
suspiciously peer
from curtained windows;
sheltering in place.

The vicious teeth of death
grins at our arrogance;
industrial waste,
hormone injected livestock,
ocean floors in plastic.

In the backyard,
Canadian gooslings
follow adults.
Fat groundhogs voraciously
eat the lawn.
Bears stalk playgrounds
and back decks.

In medieval days,
the plague dropped the sick
in the road;
hauled away in horse drawn carts.

Today, ventless trucks
cram bodies in storage,
the reek of death.

Despair follows survivors,
A hungry mouth.

❋   ❋   ❋   ❋   ❋

PUPPET PANDEMIC

I wish the dead weren't quite so loud,
one puppet said to the other.
The puppet shows
have all gone dark,
you'd never believe how many.

The sick scream by night,
dying daily.
Maybe we could pack
the puppet population
into a space station,
waiting for the virus to pass.

How can they isolate all of us?
Some puppets are homeless.
Packed into crates,
never to reappear.

It is whispered
elderly puppets
will not be treated.

The nursing homes
deliver lunch trays
to the dead.
One puppet said
Life is precious,
committing suicide.

❊   ❊   ❊   ❊   ❊

NO CAUSE

When King Lear
tells his daughter
he has given her cause
to stop loving him,
she replies
no cause. No cause.

Although he disclaims her,
calls her stranger,
banishing her from home,
with her words
a flood of love
washes over them.

The grace of love
we don't deserve
bathes us,
even as we neglect
what is most precious.

Love speaks.
No cause, my liege.
No cause.

❊   ❊   ❊   ❊   ❊

I Want to be Christiana Amanpour

Who is filming live
from the front
without combat gear.

Who stands fearless
wearing nondescript
shirt and slacks
with her microphone,
in exploding cities.

Christiana's hair
perpetually dark,
shoulder length, bangs
or she's in half veil,
her body shrouded in
white cloth.

I want to be Christiana Amanpour,
unafraid to enter
war zones, alone,
to tell the truth.

❊   ❊   ❊   ❊   ❊

IN THE MIRROR

Death
moving to safety
there he is
in the mirror,
lost warrior
drinking pain like water,
motionless,
on the edge of the cliff.

He would tell you
how it is,
if you asked.
He would report back.
As it is,
no ears follow
the sound of his breath.

He sleeps
in sand and dry leaves.
Combat boots mask
sores on his feet.
He would take them off,
If you asked.

❅   ❅   ❅   ❅   ❅

RUNAWAY OF COMMERCE

Barbie sat
in her pink Convertible Cadillac
as the engine idled
her legs so long
even ZZ Top
would be forced to conclude
she knew how to use them.

Barbie had lately
tried donating clothes
to the thrift shop
on Park road
but does anyone know
someone who
is looking for purple boots,
black stretch pants,
textured hose
with pink go-go toes?

Or, star-spangles shells.
The glamourous evening wear
of an eleven
and one-half inch doll.

No one she would ever meet
on Fufu street
while walking her
poofy white poodle, Puffy,
would care to wear.

The red rain slicker
with the matching shoulder strap.
The occasion?
A rainy day!
What nonplastic person
outside Hollywood
had such a body?

Sixty years old,
her bustline still perky
her tummy taunt,
her bottom
relentlessly refusing
to expand.

Barbie struts down
the runway of commerce,
pivots, turns around.

* * * * *

UNSCRUPULOUS POWER

While unscrupulous power
from Washington
to Walmart rages,
the free world slides into
the mythology
of thee I sing.

Those imports that knock out
U.S. economy
might be someone's concern,
when we pay only three dollars
for a shirt costing China thirty-five cents
by young women
who sleep between shifts
at their sewing machines.

How many of us in the U.S.
see those youthful faces
turning to the artificial sun
of twenty-four hour factories.

The fluorescent lights burn,
the girls keep sewing,
while unscrupulous power,
unchecked, is growing.

❋ ❋ ❋ ❋ ❋

NOT FUNNY

It's not funny, she said
to put yourself down.
Not at all.
I thought it was, he said,
to pretend I'm a clown.

No, you know it's not funny,
and not funny to you.
Someone who was afraid
told you
you were dumb.
You never have to believe
anyone.

The planet is not laughing,
bringing death to our shores.
It asks us what about life,
anyone serious?

Don't we know better;
that this disease
bringing us to our knees,
to our graves,
will not disappear.

Blame global travel,
cruise ship confinement,
shortage of masks,
ventilators, bleach.

Blame the national economy,
collapsing in sand.
It's not running for office,
it wants to shake hands.

❊   ❊   ❊   ❊   ❊

CHAPTER FIVE:

PRESENT MOMENT

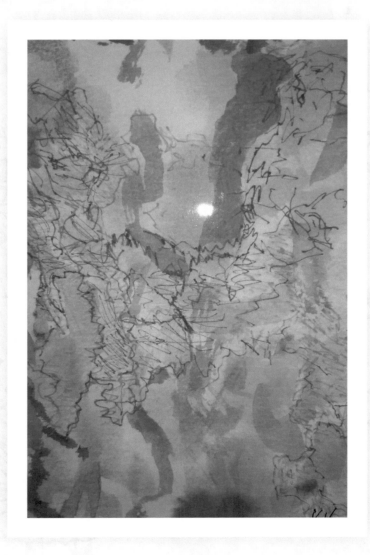

PRESENT MOMENT

PRESENT MOMENT

WELCOME TODAY

Allow fear to withdraw
from wide rooms.
Then climb inside.

Allow breath to guide you
to its center.

Fall asleep
while awake;
deepening hearing, feeling,
smell and taste.

Notice life in our breath;
the pulsing, beating,
relentless yes.

Enter the only moment
that exists;
accept the stillness,
confusion,
restlessness.

Stay for the dissolving disarray,
trust yourself.
Welcome today.

❈ ❈ ❈ ❈ ❈

TO BE KNOWN

As old as rain, the splat
of wet leaves dripping
from ancient trees
onto forest floors,
this longing to be known.

It is the lullaby of the cradle,
the piercing tears
of the grave.
This longing to be known.

Its power can cause us
to lose our way;
to craft a myth
of might have beens.

This longing
which does not agree
to stay,
but reaches, reaches
to be known.

✳ ✳ ✳ ✳ ✳

THERE IT IS

A childhood breeze
renewing trust,
a rush of heat
from inside out
stabs the chest
realizing
I am known
and, being known,
I am forgiven.

Within the imperfect hours of now,
this miracle exists,
there is always the need for allowances
and someone who cares enough
to make then for you.

A bath of light.
Perfect breath.
The ordinary shimmers
with color and energy.
Comfort
inside danger.
Ordinary. Familiar.
Oh yes, there.
There it is.

❄ ❄ ❄ ❄ ❄

LIFE SAYS YES

Life says yes, reaching
persistent arms
across indifference.

Life says yes,
take the chance,
make the move; decide.
You only risk everything
if you don't accept
your freedom.

Life exists
in the moment,
gone the next,
dissolving into new,
fragile possibilities.

The word for life is yes.

✳   ✳   ✳   ✳   ✳

THIS MOMENT

In this moment,
the pulse of life.
The heart, the lungs,
fingers, thumbs,
eyes and ears
follow shadow and sound.

From the window's
other side;
the water, the grass,
the leaves collecting
between the rocks,
a paper plate rolling
across the lawn.

A child searching
for something gone.

* * * * *

OPEN HANDS

Awaken from the nihilistic view
there is nothing you can do.
See the breath in front of you.
Soon through.

From our trance,
this watery sleep,
peel seaweed from
eyes and feet.

Brush away crusted sand.
Release to life
with open hands.

❋   ❋   ❋   ❋   ❋

IT IS

The velvet in your voice,
the competence
in your hands,
the slightly startled glance,
behind the confidence.

It is the way you
burst into a room;
like autumn,
like the cavalry.
It is your delight
in absurdity.

It is your listening
thoughtfulness,
like the sky.
The elasticity
you bring to time.

It is your forgiveness
of stupidity,
knowing
that we don't.
Your grand humanity.

It is all
that is wild in you
that somehow
made it through.

* * * * *

I Can Be

Floating off to sleep.
words release
like baby teeth,
and all around
this sacred space love fills
what language
shall erase.

I can be
a sheet of paper,
flying in the breeze.

I can be
the darkness
Or the underground,
Before sleep.

Riding on waves
of wordless dreams
language lives
in night sky,
all unseen.

✳ ✳ ✳ ✳ ✳

CELLOPHANE DAYS

Rare days,
wrapped in cellophane
and fluttering translucent trains,
trains swept away
by the smallest, disruptive breeze;
these days
our emptiness creates.

On such days,
standing outside of time,
dispassionately view
mortality race
ahead of us,
we may be released
from life and death.

It is the longing
staring in our eyes,
the intimate knowledge
of the nothing
that reaches in,
that allows us to recognize
cellophane days begin.

❋   ❋   ❋   ❋   ❋

HOME

Today, lightening sliced
through the canvas of the day.
First August
without you.

My body recalls
how effortlessly
we'd fall
against each other.
Before illness.

How safe the skin,
soft, fair,
everywhere bare.
Our ancient selves,
coming home.

Now, sharp rain
whips summer leaves
across roads,
thunder rumbles,
emptiness explodes.

❋   ❋   ❋   ❋   ❋

HALF WILD

She tore through the backyard,
a streak of black with lopping legs,
diving into the July forest
before she knew her name,
she was gone.

I scouted the riverbank,
thick vegetation
masking movement,
knowing her talent
for hiding far
exceeded bone hoarding.

Becoming a nondescript black ball,
she morphed into trees,
the rocks, the night.
The darkest, smallest
of darkest anythings.

But she was half wild,
a packless pup,
rescued from certain death
of anonymous indifference
by grace,
between months, days, hours, moments,
of random cruelty.

I slept that night,
dreaming her dog's face
became a wolf's.
Her dog body
a tightly muscled,
wild nomad.

I no longer hoped for her return,
instead,
sending her a shower of love
to rain on her,
welcoming, calm.

I imagined her sleeping
in perfect love,
unafraid, safe.

Much, much later
the next afternoon,
I heard her bark.
I opened the door.
I called to her.
She leapt into my arms.

❉   ❉   ❉   ❉   ❉

I KNOW YOU BEST

In darkness,
when masks of the day
are put away.
When we shed out skins.

I know you best
in darkness
the night sky brings.

The darkness of miles
of traveled tracks,
of freight cars
passing night waterways.
Of night flights of planes
over our roof, or
atmospheric announcements
of their descent.

I know you best
like lungs know breath,
like driftwood
floating home.

❊   ❊   ❊   ❊

IMPERFECT BEAUTY

My yoga teacher
lives in beauty imperfectly.

Balancing one leg,
strong and vulnerable.

Warrior one
bold, controlled.
She leads our flow,
We move to follow.

Triangles, tables,
awkward chairs,
circling suns
begin and end in stillness.

She is not Gandhi.
She is not pain free.
She owns her fallibility.

Honor our sacredness,
she teaches us.
Beauty in imperfection.

❋ ❋ ❋ ❋ ❋

THIS SACRED SPACE

This room,
where soft lamps cast
soft shadows of those
in wombs
of yoga mats.

Where strains of sax,
flute or pipe
become ribbons of light
waving through
the wild night.

Outside,
darkness, cold.
Brief days full of
uncertainty.
Inside,
the rhythm
of our breathing.

We reach beyond.
We come home.

Jai Bhagwan
whispering
as we depart.
I honor
the light and dark.

* * * * *

NO ONE DRIVING

The car grew
a nest of mice inside,
damaging the heating.

Pine needles shed
into the engine.

Sap splattered
the hood.
Sticky blots that
would not come clean.

Creeping greens
grew around
windows and locks.
Twirled around
the steering wheel.

No one driving.

* * * * *

Folded Leaf

Outside
inkblot sky
bleeds above the town.

I hear disembodied
sound of trains
across the river.
Windowpanes shake.

At night,
jet engines thunder,
lifting from runways
to anywhere.

Between the crossroads
of this empty place,
inside my bed,
I lay, awake.

Never so empty.
Never so small.
Sleep wraps me
in wild wind.

Awakening,
I find my dog,
curled into my breast;
a miracle,
a folded leaf.

✳   ✳   ✳   ✳   ✳

KATHLEEN KEENA, L.P.C., L.A.D.C.

This is Kathleen's third book. Prior to Present Moment, Perfect Moment, she wrote Adolescent Depression, Outside In, exploring the interior of teen depression and suicide. The Play's the Thing, her second book, shares her collaboration with Clark Bowlen, her late husband, as they produced college, community and independent theater.

Present Moment, Perfect Moment is a selection of poems, written by Kathleen Keena, over many years.

They reflect her life issues and experiences, and celebrate the present moment as our only reality.

✳   ✳   ✳   ✳   ✳

Printed in the United States
By Bookmasters